Looking at . . . Troodon

A Dinosaur from the CRETACEOUS Period

THE NEW **D**INOSAUR COLLECTION

For a free color catalog describing Gareth Stevens' list of high-quality books and multimedia programs, call 1-800-542-2595 (USA) or 1-800-461-9120 (Canada). Gareth Stevens Publishing's Fax: (414) 225-0377. See our catalog, too, on the World Wide Web: http://gsinc.com

Library of Congress Cataloging-in-Publication Data

Anthony, Laurence.
    Looking at-- Troodon/by Laurence Anthony; illustrated
by Tony Gibbons.
      p. cm. -- (The new dinosaur collection)
    Includes index.
    Summary: Describes the physical characteristics and probable
behavior of this slight, swift carnivore of the Late Cretaceous.
    ISBN 0-8368-1790-7 (lib. bdg.)
    1. Troodon--Juvenile literature. [1. Troodon. 2. Dinosaurs.]
I. Gibbons, Tony, ill. II. Title. III. Series.
QE862.S3A58 1997
567.912--dc21   97-555

This North American edition first published in 1997 by
Gareth Stevens Publishing
1555 North RiverCenter Drive, Suite 201
Milwaukee, Wisconsin 53212 USA

This U.S. edition © 1997 by Gareth Stevens, Inc. Created with original © 1996 by Quartz Editorial Services, 112 Station Road, Edgware HA8 7AQ U.K.

Consultant: Dr. David Norman, director of the Sedgwick Museum of Geology, University of Cambridge, England.

Additional artwork by Clare Heronneau.

Printed in the United States of America

1 2 3 4 5 6 7 8 9 01 00 99 98 97

Looking at . . . Troodon

A Dinosaur from the CRETACEOUS Period

by Laurence Anthony

Illustrated by Tony Gibbons

THE NEW
DINOSAUR
COLLECTION

Gareth Stevens Publishing
MILWAUKEE

Contents

Introducing
Troodon

Scientists believe that **Troodon** (<u>TROE</u>-OH-DON), also known as **Stenonychosaurus** (<u>STEN</u>-OH-<u>NICK</u>-OH-<u>SAW</u>-RUS), was very brainy — by dinosaur standards, that is.

But what else do they know about **Troodon**? Where, for instance, did this dinosaur live? Was it a carnivore or herbivore? And how do some experts believe it might have evolved if dinosaurs had not become extinct 65 million years ago?

But, as you will discover, size was not always everything in the prehistoric world. In fact, even though it was not big, **Troodon** may have been one of the most advanced dinosaurs of all.

Read on, and come face-to-face with this small but wily beast. Other dinosaurs were often taken by surprise when this smart creature was on the prowl!

Troodon was a small dinosaur.

And you, too, may be surprised in the pages that follow.

Big-eyed

One of the most striking features about **Troodon** must have been its large, alert eyes. They faced forward, like a cat's. This has led scientists to believe that, like a cat, **Troodon** had superb eyesight and would have been excellent at spotting its prey from a distance. Such a slender snout must also have made **Troodon**'s eyes seem bigger than they really were.

Some scientists even think that **Troodon** might have been able to see fairly clearly in twilight, at dawn, or at dusk, just like a cat can. This, too, would have been useful — perhaps for locating an unfortunate victim for breakfast or supper.

And what a slim, athletic body **Troodon** had! Experts can tell from its long, slender leg bones that it was probably fast on its feet and maybe one of the speediest dinosaurs of all!

Troodon had fairly long arms, ending in three sharp-clawed, flexible fingers. These would have been ideal for grasping at any wriggling creature.

dinosaur

A retractable claw on one toe of each foot was also handy for stabbing victims that struggled to get free from **Troodon**'s hold. And the fossilized teeth that paleontologists have found prove **Troodon** was a carnivore.

Surprisingly, although a successful predator, **Troodon** was not large in size — only about 6.5 feet (2 meters) long. It was probably a little shorter than you are when it was running along, its head level with the rest of its body.

As you can see in this illustration, **Troodon**'s neck was flexible. It could turn easily to see if anything was lurking behind it.

But Troodon had a big brain and was more intelligent by far than the most gigantic dinosaurs. In any case, it was nowhere near as bright as you are. But then, of course, **Troodon** lived long before even the very earliest humans lived.

Birdlike

Paleontologists have not been lucky enough so far to find a complete skeleton of **Troodon**.

Troodon must have been very slightly built and therefore light in weight. Lots of short, saw-edged teeth lined **Troodon**'s long, slender jaws. In fact, it had many more teeth than most other theropods.

Up to now, they have come across only a few of its bones and teeth. Nevertheless, they have been able to compare these with the remains of similar dinosaurs. This has given the experts a good idea of what **Troodon**'s skeleton would have looked like, as this reconstruction shows.

These teeth were ideally suited both to holding on to slippery prey, such as fish, and to ripping and slicing flesh. **Troodon** was certainly a carnivore.

skeleton

As you can see in this illustration, **Troodon**'s hand claws were large. In fact, its claws could probably have been used as powerful weapons.

Now take a look at **Troodon**'s sickle claws.

Now that you can see how delicate and slender the skeleton of a dinosaur like **Troodon** was, it's not hard to understand what lots of experts have come to believe: that the birds inhabiting our world are probably descended from some of the dinosaurs.

They were on one toe of each foot and were larger than the other foot claws. Special muscles made it easy for this claw to be moved up and down whenever **Troodon** needed to slash out at its prey with this built-in weapon, probably causing a nasty wound and great pain.

Bony rods held **Troodon**'s tail stiffly in position as this sharp-witted hunter ran through the Cretaceous landscape in search of a victim for its next meal.

Isn't it great to know that, even though dinosaurs became extinct 65 million years ago, some of their descendants are flying through our skies right now?

Turn the page to find out what life was like in those parts of the world where **Troodon** lived long, long ago before humans existed. Our planet Earth was inhabited by many unusual-looking creatures during that time, although a few closely resembled animals we know today.

The lost world

Take a look at this scene. It illustrates the sort of environment in which **Troodon** lived, way back in Late Cretaceous times.

There were many strange-looking dinosaurs roaming Earth then. Can you spot in this picture the tank-like **Ankylosaurus** (AN-KEY-LO-SAW-RUS) with its club tail? Dome-headed **Pachycephalosaurus** (PAK-EE-SEFF-A-LOW-SAW-RUS)? And **Parasaurolophus** (PAR-A-SAWR-OH-LOAF-US), with its enormous head crest, through which it would bellow loudly to signal the approach of predators?

Even though it was a highly intelligent dinosaur, **Troodon** was only a small meat-eater. There were much larger beasts that Cretaceous plant-eaters found more threatening — enormous **Tyrannosaurus rex** (TIE-RAN-OH-SAW-RUS RECKS), for example.

It was during Cretaceous times that flowering plants, such as magnolias and roses, first appeared. Willow trees, holly bushes, and sycamores dotted the landscape. Birds (some resembling today's terns and herons), snakes, and small tree-shrews also lived during this time. But there was no grass on our planet yet.

# of Troodon

Could **Tyrannosaurus rex** be in the distance, camouflaged among the trees of the forest?

Day and night, other Cretaceous dinosaurs had to be on guard constantly, just in case a creature like **Tyrannosaurus rex** was out for the kill.

Nocturnal

The full moon shone brightly, lighting up the edge of the Cretaceous forest.

On one such night, a pack of hungry **Troodon** searched for a meal of freshly caught meat. Silently, the **Troodon** lurked near some thick bushes, keeping an eye out for unsuspecting prey.

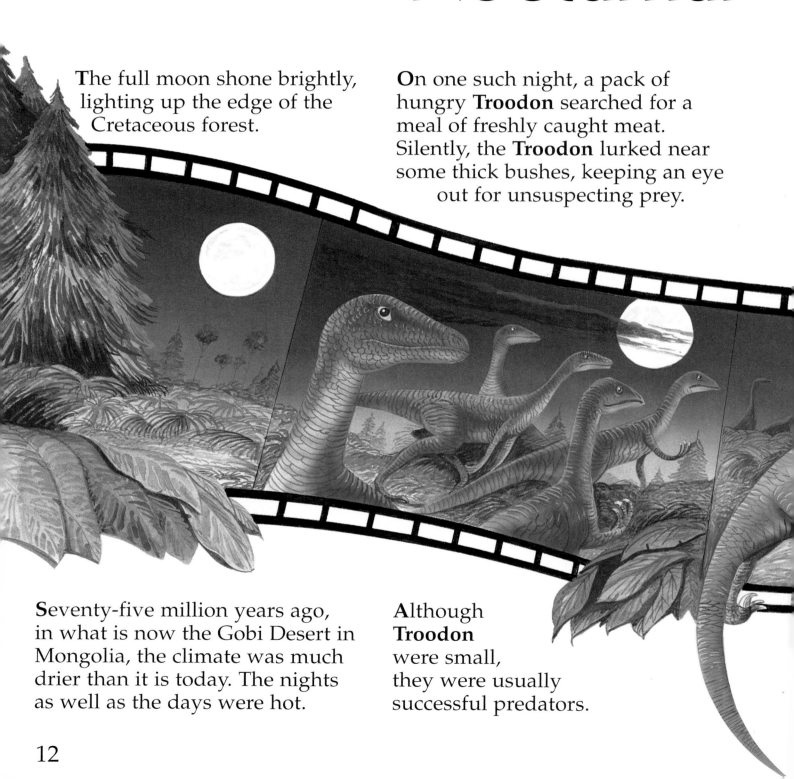

Seventy-five million years ago, in what is now the Gobi Desert in Mongolia, the climate was much drier than it is today. The nights as well as the days were hot.

Although **Troodon** were small, they were usually successful predators.

hunters

Whenever clouds passed over the moon, the forest would darken. But this was not a problem for the **Troodon**. They had excellent eyesight, even in poor light. With all their senses alert, they were bound to spot a likely victim before too long.

It, too, was a speedy and awesome predator. But what chance did it stand against an entire pack of intelligent **Troodon**?

Quick as a flash, the **Troodon** circled their victim and began to attack with their sickle claws. **Velociraptor** had claws like these, too, and a vicious battle began. But the encounter was soon over.

Suddenly, a rustling could be heard in the bushes. A lone **Velociraptor** (VEL-AH-SI-RAP-TOR) was also on the prowl.

The **Troodon** could now enjoy a meal of **Velociraptor** meat.

Dinosaur

Other carnivores — such as the **Megalosaurus** (<u>MEG</u>-A-LOW-<u>SAW</u>-RUS) shown *below* — had larger, almost fanglike teeth. Curved and pointing slightly backward to get a better grip, each tooth was a fearsome weapon. And if a tooth wore down or broke off, a new one would grow in its place. In fact, the teeth of such giant meat-eaters were constantly being replaced.

Troodon's name, given by the American scientist Joseph Leidy, means "wounding tooth." However, as you can see from the illustration *above*, this dinosaur had a very small head, and its teeth were certainly not large. In fact, remains show that **Troodon**'s teeth were not much bigger than the front teeth of an adult human today. But these teeth were sharp and partly serrated like a steak knife — just right, in fact, for slicing a victim's raw flesh.

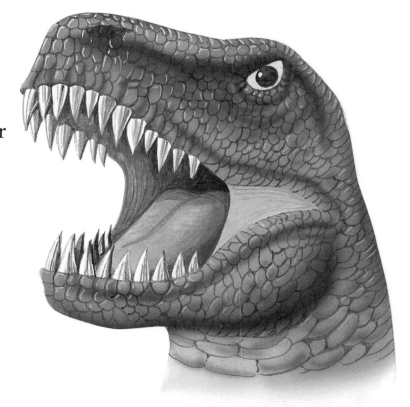

teeth

Armored plant-eaters — such as **Ankylosaurus** (AN-KEY-LO-SAW-RUS), *below* — had leaf-shaped teeth far back in their mouths that were also good for a diet of vegetation. These teeth were in their cheeks, behind a toothless beak that was ideal for snapping off tough stalks and branches.

Herbivorous dinosaurs had very different teeth from the carnivorous dinosaurs. They did not eat meat, so they had teeth that were more suited to biting off and chomping on vegetation. Enormous, long-necked, small-headed **Diplodocus** (DIP-LOD-OH-KUS), *above*, for example, had fringes of pencil-like teeth at the front of its mouth only. These teeth had to cope with enormous quantities of plant food every day.

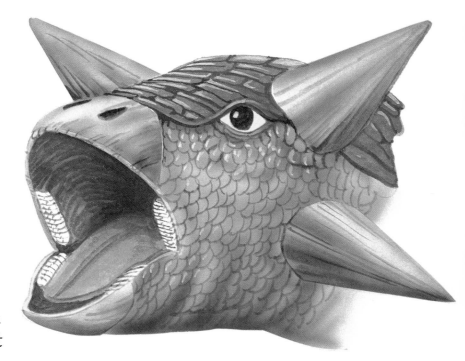

15

Dinosaur Provincial

Just imagine going for a stroll and stumbling over some dinosaur remains! How exciting that would be! It could happen if you are ever lucky enough to visit a place called Dinosaur Provincial Park in southern Alberta, Canada. The remains of **Troodon** were first discovered there by paleontologists in 1856.

New dinosaur discoveries are being made in this area all the time. About 350 skeletons of 35 different species have been dug up there so far, as well as millions of isolated bones, teeth, eggshells, and a few footprints. In fact, if scientists collected all the remains in Dinosaur Provincial Park, it would be hard to find a place big enough to display or store them.

Park

So only what scientists consider to be the best skeletons are now removed.

Paleontologists work hard to uncover dinosaur remains, and most of the skeletons they find are of larger dinosaurs. This is because the bones of larger dinosaurs were stronger, remaining almost whole over millions of years. The bones of smaller dinosaurs, meanwhile, were lighter and broke up more easily, disintegrating with time.

Many plant fossils have also been found in Dinosaur Provincial Park. These show us that, in Cretaceous times, there were both conifers and deciduous trees in what is now North America, and that the vegetation was plentiful.

Thousands of fossilized insects and other crawling creatures, such as spiders, have also been preserved in amber in Dinosaur Provincial Park. Many specimens seem to have been just like those that exist today.

How intelligent were

We know from their fossilized remains that many dinosaurs were huge. But this does not mean they had big brains and were intelligent. No dinosaur brains survive; brain tissue is too soft to become fossilized. Even so, paleontologists have obtained an accurate picture of dinosaur brains by studying the braincases of dinosaurs. The least intelligent dinosaur of all, most scientists agree, was probably **Stegosaurus** (<u>STEG</u>-OH-<u>SAW</u>-RUS) (**1**).

Stegosaurus's brain was only the size of a walnut — tiny in comparison with the bulk of this enormous herbivore's plated body. Sauropods such as **Apatosaurus** (A-<u>PAT</u>-OH-<u>SAW</u>-RUS) (**2**) were very tall, but their brains were small, too.

2

1

the dinosaurs?

So **Apatosaurus** would not have done well in an intelligence test, either. The fearsome carnivore **Tyrannosaurus rex** (3) had a brain that was actually larger than a human's. But the part used for thinking — the cerebrum — was tiny. Other sections of the brain were bigger and helped this predator hear and smell. No wonder it was such a successful hunter!

But the "best" dinosaur brains of all belonged to much smaller, fast-footed, agile hunters such as **Troodon** (4). **Troodon** was a fraction of the size of the other dinosaurs shown here, but very crafty and smart by nature. It was probably the most intelligent of all the dinosaurs, but still nowhere near as smart as *you*! Dinosaur size was not an indicator of intelligence.

3

4

Fearsome sickle-

Some dinosaurs had their own built-in fighting equipment. These were weapons such as horns, tail-clubs, or large claws. Sickle claws were particularly nasty because they were not visible at first. They were usually retracted, or held back, and extended quickly when the need arose. **Utahraptor** (<u>YOO</u>-TAH-<u>RAP</u>-TOR) **(1)**, whose remains were found recently in the United States, was 23 feet (7 m) long and had magnificent sickle claws.

clawed dinosaurs

Velociraptor (VEL-<u>AH</u>-SI-<u>RAP</u>-TOR) (**2**), native to China, Mongolia, and Eastern Europe, was also a sickle-clawed carnivore but much smaller.

Larger **Deinonychus** (<u>DIE</u>-NO-<u>NIKE</u>-US) (**3**), whose name means "terrible claw," lived in what is now western North America and was also a carnivore, with sickle claws designed to be nasty weapons.

And there was **Troodon** (**4**), of course. It had a sickle claw on each hind foot, but these were nowhere near the size of the sickle claws of a dinosaur as big as **Utahraptor**. Even so, **Troodon**'s claws were effective when hunting for a meal of raw steak.

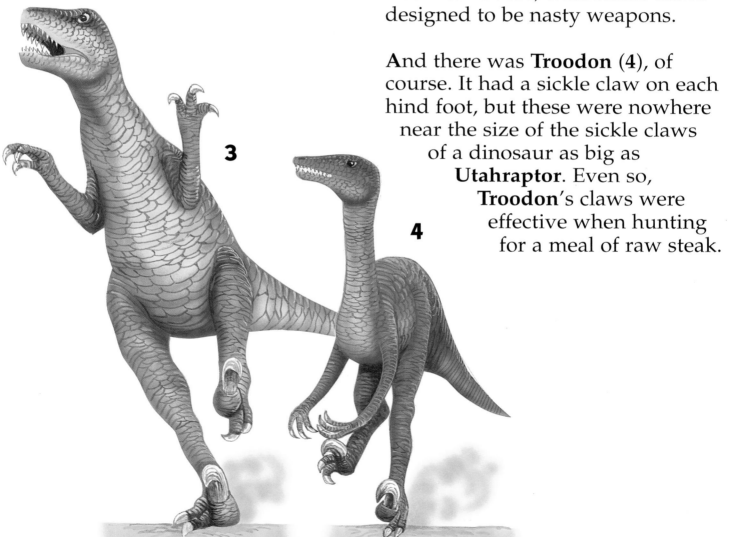

Troodon data

Troodon was an unusual dinosaur. Some experts have suggested that it might even have evolved to be humanlike, with an upright posture, if it had not become extinct with all the other dinosaurs about 65 million years ago.

Paleontologists Dale Russell and R. Sequin built a model showing how they think **Troodon** might have evolved over millions of years. This model is now on display in the National Museum in Ottawa, Canada, and resembles the extraordinary figure shown in this illustration.

The two scientists gave this imaginary creature the fantasy name *Dinosaurid* (<u>DINE</u>-OH-<u>SAW</u>-RID). But other scientists disagree with them and think **Troodon** would never have evolved to become at all like humans in appearance or behavior. What do *you* think about this possibility?

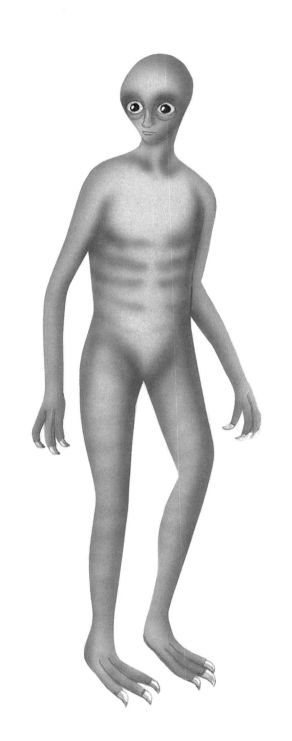

Serrated teeth

Troodon teeth were first found by the American scientist Ferdinand V. Hayden in 1855. Since then, paleontologists have discovered many **Troodon** teeth in western North America, Mongolia, and Transylvania (in Eastern Europe). Its teeth were small but clearly the teeth of a meat-eater because they were serrated, like a steak knife. This meant they were ideal for ripping flesh.

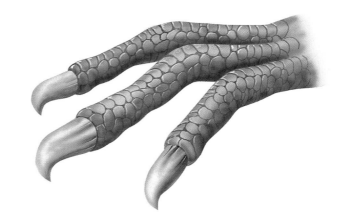

Clawed forelimbs

Troodon was not big, but it had large claws on its forelimbs. These were strong and must have helped this small, sly carnivore get a good grip on its prey.

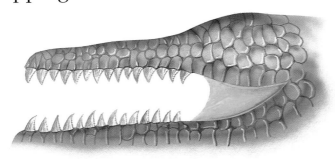

Big brain

We know **Troodon**'s brain was big because scientists have found the fossilized remains of a bone casing that once contained a **Troodon** brain. The brain itself, however, had disintegrated over time.

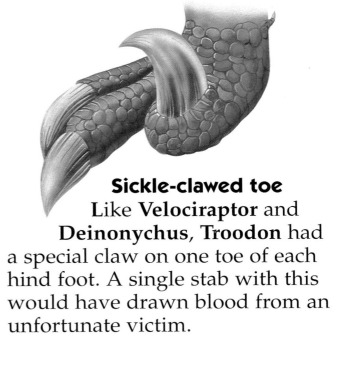

Sickle-clawed toe

Like **Velociraptor** and **Deinonychus**, **Troodon** had a special claw on one toe of each hind foot. A single stab with this would have drawn blood from an unfortunate victim.

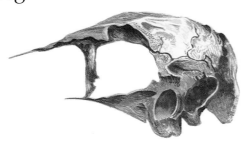

GLOSSARY

amber — the hard, clear, brownish-yellow fossil resin of extinct conifers.

carnivores — meat-eating animals.

evolve — to change shape or develop gradually over a long period of time.

extinct — no longer alive.

fossils — traces or remains of plants and animals found in rock.

herbivores — plant-eating animals.

paleontologists — scientists who study the remains of plants and animals that lived long ago.

predators — animals that kill other animals for food.

prey — animals that are killed for food by other animals.

remains — a skeleton, bones, or dead body.

sauropods — gigantic, plant-eating dinosaurs with strong legs, long necks, and small heads.

theropods — meat-eating dinosaurs that walked on their hind legs. **Troodon** was a theropod.

INDEX